Today's Superstars
Entertainment

Cameron Diaz

by Geoffrey M. Horn

GARETH STEVENS
GS
PUBLISHING

A Member of the WRC Media Family of Companies

Please visit our web site at: www.garethstevens.com
For a free color catalog describing Gareth Stevens Publishing's
list of high-quality books and multimedia programs, call
1-800-542-2595 (USA) or 1-800-387-3178 (Canada).
Gareth Stevens Publishing's fax: (414) 332-3567.

Library of Congress Cataloging-in-Publication Data

Horn, Geoffrey M.
    Cameron Diaz / by Geoffrey M. Horn.
      p. cm. — (Today's superstars. Entertainment)
    Includes bibliographical references and index.
    ISBN 0-8368-4231-6 (lib. bdg.)
    1. Diaz, Cameron—Juvenile literature. 2. Motion picture actors
and actresses—United States—Biography—Juvenile literature. I. Title.
PN2287.D4633H67   2005
791.4302'8'092—dc22
[B]   2005042670

This edition first published in 2006 by
Gareth Stevens Publishing
A Member of the WRC Media Family of Companies
330 West Olive Street, Suite 100
Milwaukee, WI 53212 USA

This edition copyright © 2006 by Gareth Stevens, Inc.

Editor: Jim Mezzanotte
Art direction and design: Tammy West
Picture research: Diane Laska-Swanke

Photo credits: Cover, © Frank Micelotta/Getty Images; pp. 5, 7, 21, 23, 24
Photofest; p. 11 © Marion Curtis/DMI/Time & Life Pictures/Getty Images; p. 13
© Chris Weeks/Getty Images; p. 15 © DMI/Time & Life Pictures/Getty Images;
p. 17 © Vince Bucci/Getty Images; p. 18 © Getty Images; p. 26 © Junko Kimura/
Getty Images; p. 28 © Gregg DeGuire/WireImage.com

Printed in the United States of America

1 2 3 4 5 6 7 8 9 08 07 06 05

Contents

Chapter 1

Smokin'!

In the movie business, whole careers can be launched with a single scene. Consider *The Mask*, (released in 1994) which stars Jim Carrey as a bank clerk named Stanley Ipkiss. Anyone who loves that film recalls the first time Ipkiss puts the green mask on his face. The mask wraps itself around his head, and he spins like a tornado. When the whirling stops, he grins wickedly at the camera and says, "Smokin'!" It's a perfect Jim Carrey moment.

There's another smokin' moment earlier in the film. It's the scene where twenty-one-year-old Cameron Diaz makes her very first appearance on screen. She's playing Tina Carlyle, a singer at the Coco Bongo Club.

Dazzling a Critic

A lot of film critics noticed Cameron in *The Mask*. Roger Ebert is one of the nation's best-known critics. He said, "Cameron Diaz is a true discovery in the film, a genuine sex bomb with a gorgeous face, a wonderful smile, and a gift of comic timing. This is her first movie role, after a brief modeling career. It will not be her last."

Jim Carrey and Cameron Diaz light up the Coco Bongo Club with their high-voltage dance in *The Mask*.

Rain pours down as Tina enters the bank where Stanley Ipkiss works. She is wearing a low-cut red dress. She bends down to fix a strap on one of her high-heeled shoes. In the next shot, the camera takes a long, loving look at her face. In slow motion, she shakes her blond hair from side to side.

Stanley's jaw drops as Tina walks toward him. She says she wants to open a new account. She sits down at his desk, takes his tie in her hand, and brings her face close to his. The poor bank clerk can hardly speak. He turns to the electric pencil sharpener on his desk. But it's not a pencil he puts in the sharpener — it's a ballpoint pen.

He's in love. He's so in love that he doesn't see the camera in Tina's handbag. We soon learn that she's working for a bunch of bad guys who plan to rob the bank. It looks like she's up to no good. But at this point, Stanley is too dazzled by her beauty to notice.

Fact File

Jim Carrey's mask wasn't the only special effect in *The Mask*. Cameron says the top of her dress was padded to give her a fuller figure.

Laughing at Herself

Cameron Diaz has the face and figure of a supermodel. Her smile lights up the screen. But she has more to offer than just her beauty. In the right role, she's one of the funniest people in movies today.

Cameron may be a movie star, but she is down to earth. She can cuss like a trucker, and she's not afraid to be silly. She has won several acting awards. But when a reporter came to visit her in 2002, the trophy on her desk was her Best Burp award from Nickelodeon.

In stripes and heels, Cameron still has the long, lean look of a supermodel.

Just how did she win Nickelodeon's first-ever celebrity burp war? "I chugged a Diet Coke right before going on," she says. "And then, 20 minutes later, I was walking backstage and it was like *bwaaaap*. So I thought, I've got to chug it before I get there. Be prepared! Know my lines!"

Cameron is sometimes compared with another Hollywood star, Carole Lombard. A stunning blonde, Lombard was also a great screen comic. Like Cameron, she knew how to laugh at herself. "I believe that if you can't make fun of yourself," Cameron says, "you have no business laughing at anyone else."

She admits she still has a lot to learn about being an actress. In 1997, she told an interviewer, "I learn something new about acting and about myself each time out."

Fact File

Carole Lombard starred in more than forty films from the late 1920s to the early 1940s. She was married to another famous film star, Clark Gable. She died in a plane crash in 1942, at the age of thirty-three.

California Girl

Cameron Michelle Diaz was born in San Diego, California, on August 30, 1972. Her father, Emilio, was Cuban American. Her mother, Billie, came from a mixed German, English, and Native American background. Cameron says one of her great-grandmothers was a Blackfoot Indian.

The Diaz family lived in Long Beach, a port town in southern California. Emilio worked for an oil company. Billie had a job in the export-import trade.

Cameron is grateful to her mom and dad. "I'm so blessed, so so blessed with the family that I grew up with," she says. "It's given me so much strength to be who I am.... My parents are just truly wonderful, good people."

There was a lot of laughter in the Diaz household. "My earliest memories are of laughter," she recalls. "I can shut my eyes and hear my father's laugh. My mother's laugh is even more contagious. As a child, I did everything I could to make her laugh because it would make me laugh, too."

One of the Guys

Cameron's name may have come from an old Scottish word meaning "crooked nose." The name is given to boys as well as girls. Cameron thinks one reason she got that name was because her father really wanted a boy. "I was never a daddy's girl," she says. "My dad's son, more like."

Cameron grew up tough. She learned how to take care of herself. But she also knew how to have fun. At Long Beach Polytechnic High School, she was a Polyette. The Polyettes were the school drill team. The team danced during halftime at school football games.

Fact File

Cameron has an older sister, named Chimene (sh-MAIN). "She got the Spanish name," Cameron says.

Living in Long Beach

Cameron loved growing up in Long Beach. Today, the city is the fifth largest in California. It has miles of beaches and one of the nation's busiest ports. Each year, the city gets about 345 days of sunshine.

The city's most famous landmark is the *Queen Mary*. This British luxury liner made her maiden voyage in 1936. In the late 1960s, the ship was sold. It was moved to a permanent place in Long Beach harbor. Many tourists visit the ship, which also serves as a hotel.

Cameron and her sister Chimene clown around at Radio City Music Hall in New York City.

At night, she and her friends would hit the clubs. Heavy metal and glam-rock were her favorite kinds of music.

Years later, when Cameron began making movies, people in Hollywood raved about what a good sport she was. She loved fast cars. She could hold her own at a bowling alley or in a batting cage. "The easiest person we've ever worked with," said Peter and Bobby Farrelly, who made the movie *There's Something About Mary*.

"She drinks like a sailor," Bobby told *People* magazine in 1998. "No matter what you're doing, she's in. I don't care if you're shooting pool for money or guzzling beer, she's one of the guys."

Fact File

Cameron's favorite film as a kid was *Raiders of the Lost Ark*. She says she saw it about thirty-five times. The film came out in 1981. It was directed by Steven Spielberg and stars Harrison Ford.

Skeletor

Cameron was a skinny kid. She was so thin, her classmates nicknamed her "Skeletor." Skeletor was a bony-faced villain in the TV cartoon series *He-Man and the Masters of the Universe*. When she was teased, she gave as good as she got. "I got in a lot of fights when I was a kid," she admits.

She's come a long way since her "Skeletor" days, but Cameron still knows how to have a good time. Here she poses with her Best Burp award from Nickelodeon.

Chapter 3

Good Times

Here's the scene. You're a fresh-looking teenage girl at a Hollywood party. A sleazy guy comes up to you, offering you a drink. "Heyyy, baby," he says. "You a model? You wanna be one?" You can tell in a heartbeat that your career isn't what's on his mind.

When Cameron Diaz began going to Hollywood clubs, she met a few sleazy guys. Maybe more than a few. But when she was sixteen years old, she met a man at a party who was different. He was a photographer named Jeff Dunas.

Like the others, Jeff told Cameron that she should try modeling. But unlike the others, he didn't try to hit on her. Instead, he handed her his business card. He told her, "Have your parents give me a call."

Stuck on You

Billie and Emilio Diaz trusted their teenage daughter. But they also wanted to make sure she could defend herself. Cameron remembers when Billie gave her a hairpin. The hairpin was silver, with a very sharp point. "You can use this for your hair," Billie told Cameron. "And you can use it as a weapon, too!"

Cameron was a young fashion model when this photo was taken.

15

The next day, Cameron talked with her mom. "Do you want to do it?" her mother asked.

"I don't know," Cameron answered.

"Well, you want to check it out?"

"Yeah. Can't hurt."

A week later, Cameron signed with the Elite modeling agency. Just like that, her modeling career began. Within a year, she was jetting to Japan, Australia, and Paris. She modeled for top-of-the-line clients, such as Coca-Cola. Her face appeared on the covers of national magazines. She earned thousands of dollars a day, and she had a fabulous time doing it.

Lighting Up the Set

Cameron's start in movies was almost as easy as her start in modeling. She was in her agent's office when she picked up the script for *The Mask*. She tried out for a small part, but she wound up being Jim Carrey's leading lady.

Fact File

Many stars and supermodels have worked for the Elite agency. They include Cindy Crawford, Naomi Campbell, Brooke Shields, and Demi Moore. Lauren Bush has also signed with Elite. She's the niece of U.S. president George W. Bush.

No Nude Scenes

Being a model means thinking about how you look. It also means dealing with how other people look at you. "I would sound like an idiot if I said I did not believe that people find me attractive," Cameron says.

At photo shoots, models are sometimes asked to take off their clothes. When Cameron modeled, she had no problem with the request. "If I took my clothes off during modeling, it's 'cause I made that decision then," she told film critic Betsy Pickle in 1994. But when she broke into films, she made her feelings clear: no nude scenes. Why not, she was asked. "I love my body, and I'm not afraid of it," she answered. But she wanted to make sure people were coming to see her act — not to see her naked.

In 2001, *Premiere* magazine honored Cameron and other women in the film industry.

Cameron and the rubber-faced comic had a great time making the movie. "Half the things in *The Mask* are made up right then and there," Cameron told a reporter in 1994. Carrey would clown around, she said, and "everybody would be laughing so hard."

Her next big hit was another comedy, *My Best Friend's Wedding.* In the movie, Cameron is Kimmy Wallace, a college girl with a very rich father. Kimmy is about to marry a sports reporter, played by Dermot Mulroney. His best friend is played by Julia Roberts. Julia's character decides she wants to marry him instead. She does everything she can to wreck the wedding and make Kimmy look bad.

If Kimmy were spoiled, stupid, or stuck up, the audience would root for Julia's character. But Kimmy is very nice and very smart — and very tough. In one funny scene, Julia's character tricks Kimmy into singing at a karaoke (carry-OH-kee) bar. Cameron's character sings really badly. (It takes real talent to sing so badly on purpose.) She's awful. But she's good-natured about how awful she is. She ends up seeming more lovable than ever.

Cameron improved her comic skills when she worked on the movie. She also learned a great deal by watching Julia Roberts. She saw how a woman could rule the set, Cameron said in 2005. "I learned how she could walk on set and everything would light up."

Fact File

My Best Friend's Wedding earned more than $125 million in U.S. ticket sales. It was one of the top box-office hits of 1997.

Chapter 4

There's Something About Cameron

When Cameron first read the script for *There's Something About Mary*, she says she fell off her bed laughing. The film is rated R. In this case, "R" stands for racy, raunchy, and rip-roaringly funny.

Cameron's character, Mary, is the heart of the movie. Mary is perfect in every way. She's smart. She's sweet. She's honest. She's kind. She's beautiful. She's unmarried. What more could a guy want? The joke is that Mary's perfection drives nearly all the guys around her nuts. They lie. They cheat. They steal. They make themselves look ridiculous. They're driven by an insane desire to do whatever it takes to get next to her.

Fact File

Recently, a team of doctors tested whether laughter can help keep people healthy. They found that laughter improves the flow of blood to the heart. They got people to laugh by showing scenes from *There's Something About Mary*.

Scene to Scene

A film is a series of scenes. It starts with the first scene and ends with the last scene. Many times, however, filmmakers don't shoot scenes in the order you see them. A script might call for scenes to shift back and forth between outdoors and indoors. To save money, the film crew might shoot all the outdoor scenes first. Then, the crew might move to a Hollywood set to shoot all the indoor scenes.

In a TV interview in 2005, Cameron said she loved almost everything about acting in movies. But one thing that really bothered her was jumping back and forth from scene to scene. She felt she never really understood the role she was playing until she finished the shoot. "At the end of the movie," she said, "you're like: Can I do it again, please? Let me play it. I know what I'm going to do now. I know how to play the character. I know what her story is. I know how to do this now. Give me another chance!"

Matt Dillon and Cameron were a real-life couple when they acted together in *There's Something About Mary.*

Cameron tried to be a good sport while working on the film. But she was worried about one wildly outrageous scene. Peter and Bobby Farrelly, who made the movie, understood her concern. They admitted that if the scene didn't work, it could harm her career.

"We had to meet with her a couple of times," they recalled. "We said, listen, we'll test it, and if it's not extremely funny and acceptable, we'll cut it. But we have to try it.… We were positive it would work!"

Work Hard, Play Hard

There's Something About Mary was a huge hit. It also earned Cameron her first major acting award. The New York Film Critics Circle named her Best Actress of 1998. She also won an American Comedy Award and an MTV Movie Award.

After *Mary*, Cameron starred in a weird and wacky movie, *Being John Malkovich*. "This is brilliant," she thought when she read the script. "I HAVE to be part of this. I WANT to be part of this."

Fact File

The first three Angels in the *Charlie's Angels* TV series were Farrah Fawcett-Majors, Jaclyn Smith, and Kate Jackson.

There was nothing glamorous about her role. She wore her hair dark and frizzy. In one scene, she was tied up and locked in a cage with a chimp. The movie didn't make a lot of money. But critics raved about it, and film-savvy audiences loved it. Cameron's performance was one of her best. It caught the eye of A-list directors. Top moviemakers, such as Oliver Stone, Cameron Crowe, and Martin Scorsese, were eager to cast her in their films.

Cameron also got a call from Drew Barrymore. Drew wanted to star in a movie version of *Charlie's Angels*, a popular TV series of the 1970s. Drew would be one Angel. Cameron would be another, and Lucy Liu would be the third. The film would show all three women fighting evildoers. The stunts would be wilder than the ones in the old TV

Cameron wowed filmgoers in the wacky *Being John Malkovich.*

show — more like the stunts in James Bond films.

Drew, Cameron, and Lucy had to do many of their own stunts in the movie. Their martial arts master made them train eight hours a day, five or six days a week, for three brutal months. "Meet your new best friend — pain," he warned them.

It was the first time Cameron had ever worked out regularly. The experience changed her life. After getting in shape, she took up snowboarding and surfing. "I never knew that my body could be that powerful or be that strong and that centered," she says.

Buff and tough, Drew, Cameron, and Lucy get ready for some "Angel" action.

Angels and Ogres

Charlie's Angels was released in the summer of 2000. The movie earned a bundle of money. Its success helped make Cameron Diaz one of the highest paid actresses in Hollywood.

Three years later, the Angels were back with *Charlie's Angels: Full Throttle*. This time, the budget was bigger, but the box-office take was smaller. The reviews? Don't ask. Many critics had praised the first *Angels* film as fun pop fluff. But they thought the second one was just plain bad.

Cameron had better success with two animated features. In these films, she was heard but not seen. She did the voice of Fiona — the princess who wins the heart of an ogre — in both *Shrek* and *Shrek 2*. *Shrek* was released in 2001.

Fact File

Speaking on TV in 2005, Cameron said she felt more like Fiona than any of her other roles. "As the ogre she's most like me. Not as the princess, but as the ogre.... When I saw [the movie], I felt that my voice matched the ogre part better than it did the princess part."

Trippin'

Cameron says if she hadn't been a model or a film star, she might have been a zoologist or a marine biologist. She got the chance to show her love of both nature and travel when she hosted *Trippin'* for MTV. The series aired in spring 2005. In it, Cameron and her crew travel to some of the most beautiful places on Earth. The programs show ways to help save animals that are in danger of dying out.

Mike Myers and Cameron pose with a life-size ogre at a Tokyo photo session. They flew to Japan in July 2004 to promote *Shrek 2*.

26

The film charmed critics and audiences alike. It won the Oscar for Best Animated Feature Film. *Shrek 2* sold more box-office tickets and DVDs than any other film in 2004.

When Cameron worked on *Shrek*, she never met her co-stars, Mike Myers and Eddie Murphy. She earned about two million dollars for eight days of studio work over a two-year period. For similar work on *Shrek 2*, she made about ten million dollars.

The Hollywood Life

Like many glamorous actresses of the past, Cameron has had several famous boyfriends. She and Matt Dillon were a couple even before they co-starred in *There's Something About Mary*. "On the set, they were just two actors going about their business," Bobby Farrelly told *People* magazine. But on the weekends, "They were arm in arm and fun to be around" because they were in love.

From 1999 to 2003, Cameron and actor Jared Leto were a twosome. Since she and Leto broke up, she has been linked with

Fact File

During the summer of 2004, U.S. filmgoers paid more than $430 million to see *Shrek 2* in theaters. The movie was also a blockbuster at the video counter. Home video sales of *Shrek 2* will probably top forty million copies.

Cameron greets her fans at the 2005 Nickelodeon Kids' Choice Awards.

singer Justin Timberlake. She and Justin moved into the house she bought in December 2004. It is located in the Hollywood Hills and cost more than two million dollars.

In recent years, Cameron has acted in fewer films than she did in the 1990s. She told a reporter she's just "letting things happen as they are meant to happen, rather than feeling I have to be in a certain place at a certain time."

Time Line

1972 Cameron Michelle Diaz is born August 30 in San Diego, California.

1988 Signs a modeling contract with the Elite agency.

1994 Makes her first screen appearance in *The Mask*.

1997 Co-stars with Julia Roberts in *My Best Friend's Wedding*.

1998 Wins the Best Actress award from the New York Film Critics Circle for her performance in *There's Something About Mary*.

2000 Stars in *Charlie's Angels* with Drew Barrymore and Lucy Liu.

2001 Does the voice of Fiona in the animated film *Shrek*.

2004 *Shrek 2* is the year's biggest box-office hit.

2005 Cameron hosts *Trippin'*, a travel and nature series on MTV.

Glossary

animated features — cartoons that are full-length, like movies.

celebrity — someone famous.

contagious — able to spread from one person to another person.

directors — people who supervise the making of a movie.

export-import trade — the business of shipping goods between countries.

film critics — people who make their living by giving their opinions about movies.

karaoke — a form of entertainment in which people sing the words of popular songs to prerecorded backing tracks.

marine biologist — a scientist who studies creatures that live in the sea.

ogre — a scary or unpleasant-looking creature, or someone who acts like one.

Oscar — another name for an Academy Award, which is given out by the movie industry.

zoologist — a scientist who studies animals.

To Find Out More

Books

Cameron Diaz. Latinos in the Limelight (series).
  Kieran Scott (Chelsea House)

Marine Biologists. Scientists at Work (series).
  Julie Haydon (Smart Apple Media)

Videos

Charlie's Angels (Columbia/Tristar) PG-13

The Mask (New Line) PG-13

My Best Friend's Wedding (Columbia/Tristar) PG-13

Shrek (Universal/Dreamworks) PG

Shrek 2 (Universal/Dreamworks) PG

Web Sites

The Internet Movie Database
www.imdb.com
Facts about movies and the people who make them

RogerEbert.com
www.rogerebert.com
Movie reviews and articles by Roger Ebert, one of the
  top film critics in the United States

Index

About the Author

Geoffrey M. Horn has been a fan of music, movies, and sports for as long as he can remember. He has written more than a dozen books for young people and adults, along with hundreds of articles on many different subjects. He lives in southwestern Virginia, in the foothills of the Blue Ridge Mountains, with his wife, their collie, and four cats. He dedicates this book to Marcia (there's something about her!).